Let Go Or Stay Dragged

Affirmations for Living in Harmony

nancy delong

Let Go Or Stay Dragged

Affirmations for Living in Harmony

Written by
Nancy DeLong

Edited by
Amy Bouwer

Designed by
Jason Carey

Let Go Or Stay Dragged
Affirmations for Living in Harmony
Part Three of the Let Go Or Be Dragged Series

© 2025 Nancy DeLong
ISBN (Paperback): 978-1-941320-24-2
ISBN (eBook): 978-1-941320-25-9
First Edition, First Printing
Printed in the United States of America

Published by N. Glynn Publishing
Lake Mary, FL 32746
nancydelong.com

N. GLYNN PUBLISHING, LLC

I dedicate part three of the Let Go Or Be Dragged series, Let Go Or Stay Dragged, to everyone who reads this book. We share the human condition of pushing through life, being a reflection of others, and hiding from unresolved grief.

The sayings in this book are meant to resonate with the spirit within—the part of us that can truly let go. It means being willing to be vulnerable to the truth, to acknowledge our fears, and to walk through them.

Most of all, may we feel our connection to each other through the love we share.

For years, I heard people say, "Let go and let God." It always sounded like someone was flapping pancakes. It was annoying. One day, I realized that for me, when I did not let go, I was being dragged. "Let Go Or Be Dragged" resonates for me.

As you hold this book in your hands, feel its love energy. As you read a page, feel joy. When you come to a day with a very short saying, let it speak to the place in your heart that you have yet to honor. As you read a longer passage, may it stir passion inside of you. This book is meant to be a personal experience outside of the words on the page. The words are merely the starting point of your journey into the cosmos of your original intentionality.

At the end of the day, you only have two choices. You must choose to let go or be dragged. Sometimes it is a monumental decision. My wish is that this book inspires you to embrace the life-changing opportunity to "let go."

25 JULY
DAY OUT OF TIME

Calendars were invented to measure time so our human brains would not explode. The 400-year-old Gregorian Calendar, used today, is based on the solar cycle of Earth. For eons, people used the Mayan calendar based on the lunar cycle. There was an extra day between the last day of the year and the first. This was called the "Day Out of Time."

More recently, this day has been reignited with ceremonies dedicated to artistic expression and creativity. It is a day to pause and breathe, to practice universal forgiveness, to reflect on the past, and welcome the future. What a magnificent time to be aware!

Today, I step out of my ordinary reality into the tenth dimension where time is art. Today, I feel the timelessness and freedom of being perfectly alive. Today, I close my eyes and embrace this Day Out of Time. Today, I choose to let go.

july

26 JULY
First Day

Humanity is changing. When the chaos subsides, we will step out on the other side free of greed, war, and power struggles. We'll join together in world unity and cooperation.

27 JULY

Some days, surviving ourselves is our greatest accomplishment.

28 JULY

Today, thrive in the sunlight of the spirit. May it wash over you and bring you grace.

29 JULY

Our bodies were created to house something much more precious than skin and bones—it's home to our souls.

30 JULY

Today, realize that you have allowed the opinions of others to keep you in prison for too long. Now that you realize it, you can choose to be free of it. The cell door is open, walk out into the light.

31 JULY

Today, I will stop bleeding over people who didn't cut me. Think about it.

august

1 AUGUST

There is an infinite amount of joy in the Universe and a minimal amount of pain. So today, swim in joy.

2 AUGUST

God is not superhuman. God is God! Think about it.

Thinking of you, John Sinclair

3 AUGUST

My friend, Frank Hunnicut, had the perfect remedy for feeling sad, bad, or lonely: "He called us girls 'Chicken' and the guys 'Partner.' When I had a problem, he'd say, 'Chicken, go help someone. You'll feel a whole lot better.'" And he was always right.

4 AUGUST

Today, go to the place that makes you feel good, and revisit that place again and again and again.

Happy Anniversary, Cathy and Leo Spires

5 AUGUST

"To love and be loved is to feel the sun from both sides."

~ David Viscott

Happy Anniversary, Jenny and John Jump

6 AUGUST

"Co-creation is the connection of souls with love, compassion, and purpose," tweeted the hummingbird.

7 AUGUST

Love constantly challenges me to break my endless fixation on "me."

8 AUGUST

What are you thinking about today? Happiness, joy, kindness? Anger, resentment, revenge? Remember this. As fast as thoughts cross your mind, you can only hold onto one thought at a time. So, think happy!

Thinking of you, PJ Sutherland

9 AUGUST

Remember you are the brilliant idea of a loving essence. You are meant to flourish, to create, to be the love that heals the world.

Happy Birthday, Liam Reed Spires

10 AUGUST

I cherish each moment we spent together. These are pictures I hold dearest to my heart.

Happy Birthday, Mom

11 AUGUST

"When sleeping women wake, mountains move."

~ Chinese Proverb

Thinking of you, Debbie Macleod

12 AUGUST

The highest form of knowledge is empathy, for it requires us to suspend our egos and live in another's world.

~ Plato

13 AUGUST

"What other people think about you is none of your business—until you allow it to be," hooted the owl.

14 AUGUST

We earn our angel wings one feather at a time.

15 AUGUST

Love and grace combined are the divine alchemy of God.

Thinking of you, Paul and Amy Bakke

16 AUGUST

The only way we open up the channel to the Essence of Love is from the inside out because it's always been inside of us.

17 AUGUST

"If I had thumbs, I'd take over the world," said Spirit the Cat.

Happy Black Cat Day!

18 AUGUST

Words have power! So today say: "Imagine that" rather than "unbelievable." "Boundless" rather than "unlimited." "Remember" rather than "don't forget." "Vital" rather than "indispensable." "Appreciate" rather than "grateful." Then see how your world changes.

19 AUGUST

"Teach me to trust my heart, my mind, my inner knowing, so that I may enter my sacred space and love beyond my fear."

~ Lakota Prayer

Happy Birthday, Pampy Old Boy

20 AUGUST

Through God's grace, my mistakes become compost for a beautiful garden.

21 AUGUST

We are on the planet to support one other on a deeper level than ever before. This creates an energy shift. Be an honored part of that today.

22 AUGUST

"Love seems the swiftest, but it is the slowest of all growths. No man or woman really knows what perfect love is until they have been married a quarter of a century." (Or in some cases, even longer.)

~ Mark Twain

Happy Anniversary Jesse and Carole Pope

23 AUGUST

It's time to change this sad era when it's easier to smash an atom than a prejudice.

24 AUGUST

Today, live in the feeling of your dreams fulfilled.

25 AUGUST

"The purpose of art is to wash life's daily dust off our souls."

~ Pablo Picasso

26 AUGUST

Letting go is like jumping out of an airplane. It's scary, it's thrilling, it's freeing, but it doesn't feel safe until the parachute opens.

27 AUGUST

"The scientists of today think deeply instead of clearly. One must be sane to think clearly, but one can think deeply and be quite insane."

~ Nikola Tesla

28 AUGUST

Today, listen to the actions of those who cross your path.

29 AUGUST

"Let go of the people who are not prepared to love you. This is the hardest thing you will have to do in your life, and it will also be the most important thing."

~ Sir Anthony Hopkins

30 AUGUST

It's impossible to be spiritual and hateful at the same time. Think about it.

31 AUGUST

Our vast tapestry of memories fills in the gaps in our perceptions of the material world.

september

1 SEPTEMBER

Some days I feel the sunlight of the spirit reflected from those around me, and some days it's reflected from me.

2 SEPTEMBER

Being a free spirit, regardless of the circumstances in your life, shows impeccable strength.

3 SEPTEMBER

Remember this: Life is far more than you could possibly imagine when you decide to fully live it!

4 SEPTEMBER

Without words there are no songs. Without songs there are no tunes. Oh, but there is always music!

Thinking of you, Jason Carey

5 SEPTEMBER

Appreciate everything in your life today. If it brings you joy, keep it; if it doesn't, change it.

6 SEPTEMBER

Who am I judging today? If God loves us all perfectly from before the earth was made, then my judging anyone is like giving an open jar of glitter to a toddler. It's going to make a big mess. Oh wait, is that a judgement?

7 SEPTEMBER

Today, appreciate the challenges you face because these bring you closer to your Creator.

8 SEPTEMBER

Trudge means "walk with a purpose." Find your purpose and trudge toward it today.

Thinking of you, Loretta James

9 SEPTEMBER

I'm here on a path guided by the spiritual principles of my ancestors. I am here to love and be of service to others. But some days, my ego tugs at my coattails and wants me to think I'm in charge, that I'm the center of the Universe, and that this life is about me-me-me-me-me. Thankfully, I have a loving God to remind me of my purpose and direct me back onto the path.

Thinking of you, Mark Mathews

10 SEPTEMBER

I believe that the secret to longevity is to feel safe enough to stay curious.

11 SEPTEMBER

"Change will not come if we wait for some other person, or if we wait for some other time. We are the ones we've been waiting for. We are the change that we seek."

~ Barack Obama

12 SEPTEMBER

Treasure the disruption in your life today. It's there to get your attention so you can hear God.

13 SEPTEMBER

A resentment is like a corroded thread woven into the fabric of your life.

14 SEPTEMBER

"Nothing is more important than empathy for another human being's suffering. Nothing. Not a career, not wealth, not intelligence, and certainly not status. We have to feel for one another if we're going to survive with dignity."

~ Audrey Hepburn

Thinking of you, Amy Bouwer

15 SEPTEMBER

The only way I can be separated from God is when I think I am.

16 SEPTEMBER

Every moment, every interaction, are gifts from God. I want to really hold this in my heart today.

17 SEPTEMBER

Today, avoid being prideful about how humble you are.

18 SEPTEMBER

If you are "too much" for some people, know this: They are not your people.

Thinking of you, Fred Schott

19 SEPTEMBER

The deeper your spiritual connection becomes, the more clarity you have within your sixth sense. Trust this as you move through the day.

20 SEPTEMBER

While you're here on the planet, live every moment: Feel it! Know it! Be it!

Game on!

21 SEPTEMBER

"At the head of all understanding is realizing what is and what cannot be, and then the consoling of what is not in our power to change."

~ Solomon ben Judah, 11th Century Poet

22 SEPTEMBER

"Pain is a glacier moving through you, carving out deep valleys, and then creating something beautiful."

~ CharlieMackesy

23 SEPTEMBER

You are love! So much love that when others are with you, they are love too!!

24 SEPTEMBER

Tears are the raindrops of our souls and nothing grows without rain.

25 SEPTEMBER

"What will heal your spirit?" asked the dolphin. "Do that today!"

26 SEPTEMBER

Words are so powerful. Once spoken, they can never be unspoken.

27 SEPTEMBER

God weaves the tapestry of our lives. Whatever happens to us, he uses for our highest good.

Happy Birthday, Jill Spires

28 SEPTEMBER

How old would you be today if you didn't know what day you were born?

29 SEPTEMBER

The quality of your life is often about what you can endure in the material world. It's more important to have quality in your spiritual life. Think about it.

Thinking of you, Jared West

30 SEPTEMBER

Perhaps the common problem of all of humanity is a disconnection from God. (And he is not the one that moved.)

october

1 OCTOBER

If imagination creates reality, there is no fiction.

2 OCTOBER

I'm enthralled by the power of words spilling out of me onto the page, seemingly of their own accord.

Happy Birthday to me!

3 OCTOBER

Journaling is ritual! It allows you to connect with your higher self.

4 OCTOBER

Sometimes physical ears have a hard time hearing. So today, listen with your heart.

5 OCTOBER

"Happiness is when what you think, what you say, and what you do are in harmony."

~ Mahatma Gandhi

Happy Birthday, Sophie Jump

6 OCTOBER

Magic happens when we keep looking for what's not there.

Thinking of you, Laura Odria

7 OCTOBER

Fiercely love change! Make this a daily practice.

8 OCTOBER

"The day science begins to study non-physical phenomena, it will make more progress in a decade than in all the previous centuries of its existence."

~ Nikola Tesla

9 OCTOBER

The land, and all that moves upon it, is alive and sacred. See what exists on earth using something other than your eyes.

10 OCTOBER

Be a grain of sand on the beach of understanding.

11 OCTOBER

There is an ancient Mayan saying, "In Lak'ech Ala K'in," which means "I am you, and you are me." Imagine if we could see everyone who crosses our path with that thought.

12 OCTOBER

Here's something to ponder: The human spirit is far more powerful than anything man can make. Remember this when you are telling others how souls are created.

13 OCTOBER

Today, may I see myself and others as God made us in his perfect love.

14 OCTOBER

When you dip your toes into the deep, wild rush of everything, you discover that all you ever really wanted was to swim.

15 OCTOBER

Life is in session. Embrace it!

16 OCTOBER

Today remember, you can't make a flower grow by pulling on it.

Thinking of you, Rena Keane

17 OCTOBER

"The only real sin is a conscious separation from God." Think about it!

~ Chuck Chamberlain

18 OCTOBER

The God in you speaks to the God in me, and vice versa.

19 OCTOBER

Some days the exhilaration of living comes from feeling not ready and jumping in anyway.

Thinking of you, Vikki Rood and Ken Doner

20 OCTOBER

Today, I set aside everything I think I know about everything. May I be open to whatever comes my way and remain teachable.

Thinking of you, Deana Schott

21 OCTOBER

Our intuition flourishes as we embrace and grow our spirituality.

22 OCTOBER

"I want my people back. All. I cannot lose even one spirit, one soul. We will live again in love, kindness, generosity. We will again communicate with all living things with thought and wind telepathy. I am Lakota."

~ Wallace Black Elk
Columbus, Ohio, October 22, 1996

23 OCTOBER

The only thing you totally control is where you spend your time and energy, on what, and with whom. So today, be mindful of what you do, what you say, and with whom you share your time. Now watch your life change!

24 OCTOBER

"If there is any secret to this life I live, this is it: the sound of what cannot be seen sings within everything that can. And there is nothing more to it than that."

~ Storypeople

Thinking of you, Sue Jones

25 OCTOBER

"You are not separate individuals, you are linked in ways that you can only hope to imagine," declared the Essence.

Thinking of you, Debbie Davis. Mt. Shasta

26 OCTOBER

Today, act better than you feel. Wow, what a concept!

27 OCTOBER

Lasting change occurs through repetition. Think about it.

28 OCTOBER

Love is the only pill for the soul. Breathe that in today.

Missing you, Daddy

29 OCTOBER

What are you holding in your heart today? If it's anything but love, start the day over.

30 OCTOBER

Don't be a ghost in your own life today.

31 OCTOBER

Your love sustains me in all my endeavors.

Thinking of you, Leslie John Rafferty

november

1 NOVEMBER

Lean into all of the joyful moments today!

Thinking of you, Otto Budig

2 NOVEMBER

Besides "I love you," the most important words for a healthy relationship are: "Perhaps you're right." (Memorize that little phrase today. It will come in handy.)

3 NOVEMBER

Nourish your life with a balance of love, family, friendship, laughter, work, and play. Do you have enough sustenance for today?

4 NOVEMBER

"In America, you cannot be a patriot if you only accept the election results when your candidate wins."

~ President Joseph R. Biden, Jr.

5 NOVEMBER

Creativity flows from a spiritual energy greater than ourselves that lives within us.

Happy Birthday, Jenny Jump

6 NOVEMBER

Fate is happenstance; destiny is meant to be.

7 NOVEMBER

Remember this, we are all spirits with skin, and we're here to champion a world of peace, love, and harmony.

Thinking of you, Severn Mason-Rose

8 NOVEMBER

Heaven is anywhere God is.

Thinking of you, Paul Hoyer

9 NOVEMBER

Make today a day of love and peace. (And then, make it a daily practice.)

10 NOVEMBER

It ain't what you don't know that gets you into trouble. It's what you know for sure that just ain't so. Think about it.

11 NOVEMBER

How you see yourself changes depending on the people whom you allow into your life. So today, assess your relationships. Do they reflect who you really are?

12 NOVEMBER

Each of us is a living document. Think about it.

13 NOVEMBER

Laughter is the irresistibly contagious cure for a multitude of maladies.

14 NOVEMBER

Here's a thought: Today, I will not be a prisoner of me.

15 NOVEMBER

Our sixth sense comes through our spiritual connection. Today, may yours flourish!

Thinking of you, Felisha Higgins

16 NOVEMBER

Daily repetition of spiritual principles such as loving, caring, and being of service to others is where we discover permanent freedom from the bondage of self.

Happy Birthday, John Jump

17 NOVEMBER

What you really want in life may be lost if you focus only on what you want in the moment.

18 NOVEMBER

What is grief if not proof of love enduring?

Thinking of you, Josh Horne

19 NOVEMBER

We live in a love connection with all beings. This energy is written in the DNA of every living creature.

20 NOVEMBER

Learning is cyclic not linear. Say that again.

21 NOVEMBER

"The difference between the almost right word and the right word is really a large matter. It's the difference between the lightning bug and the lightning."

~ Mark Twain

22 NOVEMBER

Here's a thought: Today, love the God within those who harm you.

23 NOVEMBER

Like a magnificent tapestry unraveled across time's loom, sacred words provide solace to weary souls amidst life's tempestuous storms.

24 NOVEMBER

Today, go to the quiet place where you feel closest to your own heart.

Thinking of you, Shannon Klenk

25 NOVEMBER

Silence and laughter are powerful tools. Use them often and appropriately.

26 NOVEMBER

We sometimes need to get rid of old memories, habits, and past traditions that no longer grow corn for us. Only freed from past burdens can we take advantage of the present.

27 NOVEMBER

Stress is the place between how things really are and how I want them to be.

28 NOVEMBER

With how crazy the world is, it's easy to forget we can still choose love.

Thinking of you, Pam Ohab

29 NOVEMBER

Insecurity is at the root of a person's need to control everything. Think about it.

30 NOVEMBER

Life is predictable in its unpredictability. Unravel that today.

Thinking of you, Sue Dean

december

1 DECEMBER

Sometimes I think we are fierce spirit beings in fragile human shells. That's why we need each other so much for encouraging words and a cup of tea.

Thinking of you, Marilyn Horne and Janice Barnes

2 DECEMBER

I believe that the most important command of all of God's commands was: "Let there be light." It's the action we take to move out of the darkness.

Thinking of you, Charles "Buddy" Feucht

3 DECEMBER

Momentum is the currency of life — it opens the floodgates of creativity.

4 DECEMBER

It's time to come out of the shadows and share your light with the world.

5 DECEMBER

Every "I am" that I speak is what I bring into existence. So today, I will be mindful of what I say "I am" about.

6 DECEMBER

Forget mind over matter. It's spiritual world over material world.

Thinking of you, Karen Coli

7 DECEMBER

Think about this today: We open the channel to God from the inside out because it's always been inside of us.

Thinking of you, Sandy Beach

8 DECEMBER

Today, know that you are an expression of God because that is exactly who you are.

9 DECEMBER

Context is the driving force of infinity. It opens the door to remembering that we are all connected. Energetically, we are one. And more than any other time in our humanity, we need to remember this spiritual truth.

10 DECEMBER

I am not a drop in the ocean, but rather, I am the entire ocean in a drop.

Thinking of you, Shelley Hughley

11 DECEMBER

From one seed of imagination, you can create a world of courage, strength, and renewal.

12 DECEMBER

We are in a time when the young ones are learning in a new way—their way. So the task of a modern educator is to irrigate deserts rather than cut down jungles.

13 DECEMBER

God has no grandchildren, only children. Think about it.

14 DECEMBER

Today, embrace your beautiful spirit, warts and all.

15 DECEMBER

"Every saint has a past, and every sinner has a future."

~ Oscar Wilde

16 DECEMBER

Humility is asking for God's will and then accepting it.

17 DECEMBER

What heals your soul? Do that today.

18 DECEMBER

My true propensity to flourish is based on my ability to release the shackles of the false beliefs I hold against myself.

19 DECEMBER

Sometimes life is not fair. But I find that I come away with a bag of tools to help others going through similar challenges.

20 DECEMBER

Be present today. Encircle yourself in the energy you want in your life right now. Tap in! Be it!

21 DECEMBER

Graduate from striving today. Hmm, let me think about that.

22 DECEMBER

Look for the God in everyone you meet today because sometimes the goodness is buried deep.

23 DECEMBER

"Since love grows within you, so beauty grows. For love is the beauty of the soul."

~ St. Augustine

24 DECEMBER

To love someone deeply gives you strength. Being loved by someone deeply gives you courage.

25 DECEMBER

The divine alchemy of God is love and grace, combined.

26 DECEMBER

Today remember, God smiles when he thinks of you.

27 DECEMBER

Be a life-altering solution for everyone who crosses your path. How? Smile!

28 DECEMBER

External behavior is dictated by my spiritual condition, always!

29 DECEMBER

You are made of God stuff, so relax. You're doin' great!

Thinking of you, Stephanie Schott

30 DECEMBER

"Man did not weave the web of life, he is merely a strand in it. Whatever he does to the web, he does to himself."

~ Chief Seattle, Duwamish Tribe

31 DECEMBER

Infinity moves in both directions at once. When you release the past, the future opens to meet you. In every breath, you stand at the center of all that was and all that will ever be.

january

1 JANUARY

Life is in session!

❧

2 JANUARY

God comes to me disguised as my life.

❧

3 JANUARY

Today, I ask Spirit, "May I see what you want me to see, hear what you want me to hear, and be what you want me to be."

4 JANUARY

Let the God within you work without you today.

5 JANUARY

Today, be old enough to believe in fairytales again.

6 JANUARY

Resentment is a manifestation of self in the material world. It cuts us off from the sunlight of the spirit.

7 JANUARY

What "Wow!" moments do you want in your life today? Here's a hint: "Wow!" moments happen when you see with your heart.

Thinking of you, Dee Rollins

8 JANUARY

Today, I will stop projecting the idea of ill-intent onto those around me. How? I see every person, including myself, as God made us. I see all of life's events as for my highest good.

9 JANUARY

Only forgiveness can open the door to the grace of God in my life. Only willingness will keep the door open.

10 JANUARY

Love and Spiritual Law are the sustaining order of the Universe.

11 JANUARY

I have come to understand that God is a mystery, so I will never understand him—but oh, I do love him!

12 JANUARY

Today, embrace whatever happens in your life as an opportunity rather than a challenge.

Thinking of you, Kaycee Parker

13 JANUARY

A break from reality offers a shift in perception. Hmm, think about that.

14 JANUARY

When we live in the present, we rarely recognize the most significant moments as they unfold. It's only when we pause to reflect that we see the profound power they carried all along.

15 JANUARY

"There is no one you-ier than you!"

~ Sister Mary Ignatia

16 JANUARY

Today, I will not believe everything I think.

17 JANUARY

Defrag your mind today. Think about it!

18 JANUARY

Letting go absolutely is a hilarious concept to me. I believe it might happen in a moment, but it cannot be consistently maintained. It screams against my human nature. I have to be dragged before I can let go.

19 JANUARY

"The way I see it, if you want the rainbow, you gotta put up with the rain!"

~ Dolly Parton

20 JANUARY

The long thread of hope, which runs through our many lifetimes, always reappears when we need it most.

21 JANUARY

Today, create your own magic, choose wisely for yourself, and embrace the knowing that you already are that which you want to be.

Happy Birthday, Auston Boystak

22 JANUARY

Speak your truth out loud! It becomes part of the reality of the Universe.

23 JANUARY

God is not absorbed in the private affairs of a chosen few. Think about it.

24 JANUARY

Value laughter. It frees the soul.

25 JANUARY

The only way to understand inclusion is to experience being excluded. Hmm.

26 JANUARY

Let's be clear, God doesn't have to love you because he already loves you perfect. God is love. And that love energy is what you are made of.

27 JANUARY

Misunderstandings are always caused by one's inability to appreciate another's point of view.

28 JANUARY

It is not enough to recognize past trauma intellectually. We must feel it in our cells which have been blocked by the pain. Only a spiritual connection can open up those stuck places.

29 JANUARY

Today, I face my vulnerabilities and summon the courage to believe that I am worthy of love and belonging.

30 JANUARY

The quiet power within us whispers beneath our conscious thoughts. It's where reason meets instinct, and imagination dances with all that is real.

31 JANUARY

How do you want to be remembered? How will you be remembered? Do these match up?

february

1 FEBRUARY

A human spirit functions in many realities at the same time. Hmm, let me think about that.

Thinking of you, Heather Lentz

2 FEBRUARY

If you must preach, then preach on a soul level that the heart can hear.

3 FEBRUARY

Today be a fountain, not a drain.

Happy Birthday, Maddy Jump

4 FEBRUARY

Today, open your heart, and keep a loose grip.

Thinking of you, Jodilee Pope-Stanton

5 FEBRUARY

God is everything and everywhere. With repetition, I become aware that I must love God more than my pain, hurt, lack, fear, or uncertainty.

6 FEBRUARY

Today, I'm telling my subconscious mind to abort thoughts of what others think of me.

7 FEBRUARY

Today, instead of saying, "I am sad," I say, "Sadness is upon me." I use "is upon me" for any other feeling, condition, health issue, financial issue, or social situation that I do not want in my life. By making this change, I claim to the Universe that my soul is infinite and not defined by any human condition.

8 FEBRUARY

The aroma of praise is sweet, just don't inhale it.

Thinking of you, Marty Jeffery

9 FEBRUARY

Be immersed in something greater than yourself today.

Thinking of you, Alicia Pope-Myers

10 FEBRUARY

Vulnerability opens the door to connecting with others. And today, more than any time in human history, we need to be connected.

Thinking of you, Veronica Schimp

***

11 FEBRUARY

When I stay connected to my energy stream, I win. And no one loses for me to win because there is an endless supply in the stream. Hmm, think about that.

***

12 FEBRUARY

What are you running from today?

13 FEBRUARY

Just for today, stop looking to others for love they cannot give.

⁂

14 FEBRUARY

Today, may I see all people, including myself, as God made us. Wow, that's a game changer.

Thinking of you, Sue Jones

⁂

15 FEBRUARY

We are never above or below spiritual law. We are living it. And ignorance of the law is no excuse.

16 FEBRUARY

Today, be the fun-loving, precious, curious, trusting spirit you are meant to be.

Happy Birthday, Annette Pope-DiSabato

17 FEBRUARY

Only you have the power to unveil the light within you and share it with the world.

18 FEBRUARY

Part of the human condition is grieving, and grief is a very living thing. It visits us at random, unexpected moments and it has no time limits.

19 FEBRUARY

Your inner child is the wonderful, lovable, open, and authentic you. It's hiding behind the dark wall of lies, negative thoughts, and false beliefs you tell yourself. Only you can free yourself and step into the light.

20 FEBRUARY

Today, listen to your heartbeat as it merges with the universal heartbeat of the planet.

Thinking of you, Melissa Howard

21 FEBRUARY

"Always remember you matter, you're important and you are loved, and you bring to this world things no one else can."

~ Charlie Mackesy

Happy Birthday, Aiden Spires

22 FEBRUARY

Acceptance is not endorsement. Ponder that today.

23 FEBRUARY

Hold your loved ones a little closer today. Don't hold grudges—the past is the past, move on.

24 FEBRUARY

Today, find your voice and speak your words kindly.

25 FEBRUARY

You are part of a spiritual tapestry that weaves together your ancestral heritage, your current life connections, and everyone you love.

Thinking of you, Liz Archibald and Thomas Mason-Rose

26 FEBRUARY

Today, I want my skin to fit.

27 FEBRUARY

Realize your ability to help (or accept help) is your privilege, and to suffer is your choice.

Thinking of you, Warren Jennison

28 FEBRUARY

Experiences reawaken the wisdom within us.

Thinking of you, Lee Handley

29 FEBRUARY

Over the years, I have read many books with thoughts for the day, and I always felt cheated on Leap Year because there was no February 29. Was I supposed to reread February 28 again? Was I suppose to skip a day? Now, you have something to read today. You can even read February 29 the years that don't have a Leap Year. Imagine that!

"Forgive quickly. Kiss slowly. Love truly. Laugh uncontrollably. And never regret anything that made you smile."

~ Audrey Hepburn

march

1 MARCH

Face your challenges with an iron fist inside a satin glittered glove.

2 MARCH

We have the power to change the world with our stories. What's yours?

Thinking of you, Norma Merrells

3 MARCH

Before you judge your parents, remember this: You were not born with a set of directions wrapped around your umbilical cord.

4 MARCH

"I carry you with me into the world, into the smell of rain & the words that dance between people & for me, it will always be this way, walking in the light, remembering being alive together."

~ Storypeople

Happy Birthday, Daddy

5 MARCH

Without change, there would be no butterflies.

6 MARCH

It's time to find the home inside you where your inner child is nurtured and healed.

7 MARCH

The more you live in someone else's shadow, the longer it takes to cast your own.

8 MARCH

"Self-centered people cannot see three-dimensional people, only the cardboard cutouts in their minds," said the porcupine.

9 MARCH

Today, be a spearhead of God's ever-advancing creation.

10 MARCH

Research and knowledge can only take you so far—what finally resonates comes from life experience.

11 MARCH

Spiritual stuff, by definition, does not occupy time or space. Think about it.

12 MARCH

You essentially do three things in your life. Just three. Everything else you do supports these three things:

1. You make the choice to make no choice.
2. You make the choice because of fear.
3. You make the choice deliberately.

Your entire life is structured around these three choices in an infinite variety of patterns.

13 MARCH

Today, may you trust like an abandoned puppy that has been rescued.

14 MARCH

"When you release your emotional pain, your physical pain will lessen," bellowed Grandfather Bear.

15 MARCH

A grateful heart is a magnet for miracles.

Thinking of you, Amy Bakke

16 MARCH

There was a time when earthlings communicated through their thoughts. If everything is energy, then thoughts are energy. So energetically, we live for eternity through our thoughts. What are you thinking today?

17 MARCH

While we humans can't defy gravity, when we jump off the cliff, our guardian angels make sure it's a softer landing.

Happy St. Patty's Day!

18 MARCH

A resentment is like a corroded thread going through the fabric of your life. So, cut the thread.

19 MARCH

"Most people think love only looks like one thing, instead of the whole world."

~ Storypeople

20 MARCH

Today, focus on people you want to help rather than people you want to impress.

21 MARCH

When your lesser heroes die, your great ones will emerge.

22 MARCH

The Lakota have no word for "goodbye" because life is forever. We are all one heart, mind, and body.

23 MARCH

There is no such thing as a long time ago. There are only cherished memories that we hold in our hearts.

Happy Birthday, Jesse Pope

24 MARCH

Before we are born, we sign a spiritual contract that outlines what our Earth Life is meant to look like. Then, we land in reality.

Thinking of you, Mike Horne

25 MARCH

Today, put character before comfort. Think about it.

26 MARCH

Every negative thought you harbor toward yourself or someone else is your ego pressing against your divine spirit and shutting you off from the grace of God.

27 MARCH

People can be opinionated and wrong, but never in doubt.

28 MARCH

Experiences reawaken the wisdom inside us.

Thinking of you, Leslie Cox

29 MARCH

We choose our conflicts. In this lifetime, I can choose to allow others their opinions without embracing them or inflicting mine on them. This is one of the many gifts of discernment. Think about it.

30 MARCH

Heal yourself. Healed people do, in fact, heal others.

Thinking of you, Shirley Nelson

31 MARCH

Today, may the essence of love shine a light on your path that you could not yet see.

april

1 APRIL

We all know that light travels faster than sound. That's why certain people appear bright until you hear them speak.

2 APRIL

Today, release the need to blame anyone for any of the circumstances in your life, including yourself.

3 APRIL

Our greatest shame becomes our greatest ministry.

4 APRIL

"Our lives begin to end the day we become silent about things that matter."

~ Dr. Martin Luther King, Jr.

5 APRIL

Remember this: When you shine your light and someone cannot see it, it's because he must first shine his own.

6 APRIL

When I am a reflection of whoever I'm with, I can never be the person God created me to be.

7 APRIL

Today, are you nurturing your spirit or stifling it?

8 APRIL

Some people dance in the rain! Others just get wet.

9 APRIL

Shared sorrow becomes lighter, and shared joy becomes infinite. Think about it.

10 APRIL

Did you squander the hours today, or did you embrace them with joy?

_____

11 APRIL

Thankfully, God "interferes" in my life without my permission.

Thinking of you, Polly Pistole

_____

12 APRIL

Today, open the door to your spiritual heart.

13 APRIL

There's a big difference between maintaining and growing—so today, grow!

∗

14 APRIL

"For beautiful eyes, look for the good in others; for beautiful lips, speak only words of kindness; and for poise, walk with the knowledge that you are never alone."

~ Audrey Hepburn

Happy Birthday, Carole Pope

∗

15 APRIL

Today, use your stumbling blocks as stepping stones. Think about it.

16 APRIL

When you give your heart to life, it is not lost; for a thousand hearts will come back to you, and each one will contain a bit of your own.

Leslie John Rafferty, I miss you still.

17 APRIL

Today, may the beauty and joy of God resonate in your heart.

18 APRIL

Nostalgia is the twinge in our hearts for a place we ache to revisit that can never be again.

19 APRIL

If you don't do the "do," who will? Every idea chooses someone willing to bring it to life.

20 APRIL

Creativity has a life, a breath, a rhythm of its own as it joyfully flows through you.

21 APRIL

Stop believing your life is flawed. It's just life, and it belongs to God.

22 APRIL

"Treat the earth well: it was not given to you by your parents, it was loaned to you by your children. We do not inherit the Earth from our Ancestors, we borrow it from our Children."

~ Native American Proverb

Happy Earth Day

23 APRIL

Whatever you do in darkness will always come to light. Think about it.

24 APRIL

Families may be scattered by life's demands, but the love in your hearts is always your constant home.

25 APRIL

Remember this, the Universe corresponds to the nature of your song. What are you singing today?

⁂

26 APRIL

"Forgiveness is the fragrance of the violet which still clings to the heel that crushed it."

~ Anonymous

⁂

27 APRIL

Release all that you have been holding for others that is not yours to hold. Lean in. Let go. Allow the energy to flow back to you.

Thinking of you, Chris Parker

28 APRIL

Here's a thought: Actually believe what you are saying.

29 APRIL

God allows your heart to break only long enough to open it up.

30 APRIL

Am I being the I AM that I am? Now that's one to think about until it sinks into your heart.

may

1 MAY

Remember this: It's exhausting to think we can change things we cannot change.

2 MAY

Each soul has its own melody that can be heard in the whispers of the wind.

3 MAY

Like yourself more today than yesterday.

4 MAY

Your authenticity comes through your spirit, not your ego.

5 MAY

Honor the power of Nature. Flow with the rhythms of the earth, feel the coolness of evening tide and the warmth of the sun, breathe in the crisp wind of winter and the fragrance of the autumn trees, watch the sunrise.

Thinking of you, Valerie Schulz

6 MAY

"If art is not spiritual, it suffers from our human limitation."

~ Richard Wagamese, Ojibway, Ontario, Canada

7 MAY

As a writer, words are the air I breathe. They support and sustain me. They are my energy. They are my happy place. I often see words floating in the ether, looking for a place to land in the material world. And some days, these words come through me onto the page.

Message from my heart to yours!

8 MAY

"You can't depend on your eyes when your imagination is out of focus."

~ Mark Twain

9 MAY

What are you carrying in your spirit today?

Thinking of you, Susan Struebing

10 MAY

Words are so powerful. Once spoken, words can never be unspoken. So saying "my life" is incorrect. It's life, and it belongs to God. And so does absolutely everything else. Think about it.

11 MAY

All the knowledge in the world will not fill the empty hole inside you.

12 MAY

Friends are the family we choose for ourselves.

Thinking of you, Becky and Clint Biggers

13 MAY

Here's a thought: Resist less rather than try harder.

14 MAY

When all else fails, follow directions.

15 MAY

"There are no facts, only interpretations."
~ George Bernard Shaw

Thinking of you, Steve Szabo

16 MAY

Today, be thankful you have a heart so you can love and a family so you can practice.

17 MAY

"Search for yourself, by yourself. Do not allow others to create your path. It's your road and yours alone. Others might walk it with you, but no one can walk it for you."

~ Native American Code of Ethics 1994

18 MAY

Today be the least disturbed person in the room.

19 MAY

Today, be the channel through which God's gifts can flow.

Thinking of you, Abimbola Francis Lewis

20 MAY

"Feel each moment of your life as upbeat or neutral. What you may think of as a moment of failure can, in fact, be a moment of gathering strength. This mind trick will alter your life's orbit," whispered the wind.

21 MAY

Living by higher principles sometimes requires gently speaking your truth instead of running away from it.

22 MAY

What brings you bliss? Do that today.

23 MAY

Some people have brilliant minds, but they're not plugged in to anything.

24 MAY

Today, be part of something bigger than you can be alone.

25 MAY

God lifts me up with his indelible harmony, and as I listen to this music of the spheres, now and again, those heavenly chords remind me that the great composer loves me perfect.

Thinking of you, Vikki Rood

26 MAY

Having knowledge will not fill the empty hole inside you. Ponder that today.

27 MAY

Kindness is not a bonus you give to the deserving, but a debt you owe to all.

Thinking of you, Christina Carvalho

28 MAY

Many have a bit of cowardice about speaking the truth. So today be brave. Find your voice, and speak your truth.

29 MAY

What you refuse to address, you endorse.

30 MAY

Today, create your own magic. Love yourself, embrace perfect health for yourself, choose wisely for yourself, and show love and kindness to everyone who crosses your path.

31 MAY

Ponder this: You are as spiritually fit as the things that bother you.

june

1 JUNE

Today, live your life with God—Grace Over Drama.

2 JUNE

An energetic shift removes negativity, making room for treasures to be unfurled. Lean in!

Thinking of you, Sharon Rose

3 JUNE

Some days, I may not see the light, but I sure can feel the heat.

4 JUNE

Today, thank those who have shared their beauty with you so that you could find your own.

5 JUNE

Life is like a bookmark. Sometimes we put it in the book because we're not ready to read more.

6 JUNE

Today, honor the vibrancy of your spirit.

7 JUNE

Don't worry about the people in your past; there's a reason they didn't make it to your future.

_·_

8 JUNE

Oh, Great Spirit, only for so short a while you have loaned us to each other, because we take form in your act of drawing us, and we take life in your painting us, and we breathe in your singing us."

~ Aztec Indian Prayer

Thinking of you, Deidre Mackey

_·_

9 JUNE

As we value others, they respond with greater compassion and empathy. Hmm, let me think about that.

10 JUNE

Our power is perfected in weakness. Now that's a concept!

11 JUNE

We may have different religious beliefs, but our faith abides in the same omnipotent presence. When we light our flames together, we banish darkness from the world.

12 JUNE

Hate is speechless in the face of love. It only has a voice amid dysfunction.

Thinking of you, Karen Coli and Linda Lou Bradley

13 JUNE

"I release you, my beautiful and terrible fear. I release you. You were my beloved and hated twin, but now, I don't know you as myself."

~ Joy Harjo, Muscogee Nation

14 JUNE

The exciting part of solving a mystery is the not knowing. It's what makes the journey memorable.

15 JUNE

"Other things may change us, but we start and end with the family."

~ Anthony Brandt

Happy Birthday, Leo Spires

16 JUNE

"What do I have to do to see miracles?" she asked.

"Keep your eyes opened," answered the hawk.

17 JUNE

Memories are like stars in the dark night of sorrow. Time softens the pain until all that remains is the beauty of the memories and the love — Always the love.

18 JUNE

You can only heal what you are willing to feel.

Thinking of you, Darcy Cox

19 JUNE

Today, remember this, your smile lights up someone's world.

Thinking of you, Misty Armour

20 JUNE

"It does not require many words to speak the truth."

~ Chief Joseph

21 JUNE

For some, it takes a lifetime to learn that you belong to yourself.

Thinking of you, Bobbi Jo Matson

22 JUNE

You cannot antagonize people and have a positive influence on them at the same time.

23 JUNE

Life is meant to be more than a wearisome, unbroken climb over endless bridges and ridges. So, choose to live life joyfully one day at a time.

Thinking of you, Darlene Pope

24 JUNE

"Change comes when you realize the reality of what happened, has happened. It's over, in the past, and nothing can be done about it. And then, doing something about it," chattered the squirrel.

25 JUNE

"By the time you think you have no choice, you have already made a choice," chirped the beautiful red Cardinal.

26 JUNE

My ego cannot control me in a spiritual environment. Wow, some days that's tricky.

27 JUNE

Life is not an event. It's always a process. Think about it.

28 JUNE

"It is by the goodness of God that in our country we have those three unspeakably precious things: freedom of speech, freedom of conscience, and the prudence never to practice either of them."

~ Mark Twain

29 JUNE

Today, may you be filled with happiness and surrounded by all that matters to you most.

30 JUNE

"History is a narrative; it's a collection of stories sanctioned by the ruling power, and reinforced through words and images that suit them."

~ Kent Monkman, Canadian First Nation

july

1 JULY

"A good leader takes a little more than his share of the blame and a little less than his share of the credit."

~ President John Adams

2 JULY

America is more than an idea. It is an argument, a battle, between our best and worst angels.

3 JULY

Duty and service are more important than any words on a page. The authentic truth is that duty and service are the foundation of our capacity to love one another.

4 JULY

It's not enough to believe in the American Dream — we must be worthy of it.

5 JULY

"Patriotism means to stand with the country. It does not mean to stand with the President."
~ President Theodore Roosevelt

6 JULY

"Suppose you were an idiot, and suppose you were a member of Congress. But I repeat myself."
~ Mark Twain

7 JULY

When we have the courage to lose sight of the shore, we discover new oceans. Think about it.

8 JULY

"There are a thousand ways to say "no," but there is only one way to say "yes." When you choose "yes" with your whole being, it becomes the most spiritual word in the universe. And your entire world changes."

~ Richard Wagamese, Ojibway, Ontario, Canada

9 JULY

May your vulnerability show your true feelings to the world. May raw moments of honesty crack open your heart.

Happy Birthday, Grandma Grace

10 JULY

It's not enough to pull the weeds in your garden, you must plant flowers for it to flourish. Focus on your garden today.

11 JULY

"All of us share this world for but a brief moment in time. The question is whether we spend that time focused on what pushes us apart, or whether we commit ourselves to an effort—a sustained effort—to find common ground, to focus on the future we seek for our children, and to respect the dignity of all human beings."

~ President Barack Obama

12 JULY

Today, be responsible for living your life. Think about it!

13 JULY

Love your enemies. It will drive them crazy.

14 JULY

"A people that values its privileges above its principles soon loses both."

~ President Dwight D. Eisenhower

15 JULY

"Power doesn't corrupt people, it just reveals who they truly are."

~ James Riddle Hoffa

16 JULY

The grand path through your life is the path you are on, and you are always on the right path.

Happy Birthday, Hot Dog Nellie

17 JULY

The difficult part for us is not the letting go, but rather, saying goodbye to what is already gone.

18 JULY

Surrender is a gift, not a negotiation. It's the starting point of yielding my will to a power greater than myself.

19 JULY

Too often, we see the world as we want it to be, rather than as it is.

20 JULY

We are all part of the human family—spiritual, ancient, perishable, and everlasting. It injures our souls to forget that, even for a moment.

21 JULY

Once all of creation sees itself as one, we will begin again, like breathing in and breathing out and breathing in again.

22 JULY

When you open your heart, the whole wide world is yours.

Happy Birthday, Cat DeLong Spires

23 JULY

Turn up the volume of your life. Life is big. This is it!

24 JULY

Love will always, always, always bring us home.

Now
Start
Again!

FINAL NOTE

I believe that moving out of the Piscean Age (Will and Power) into the Aquarian age (Love and Harmony), is not a linear moment in time. Rather, it has a fluidity of its own, a powerful energy shift. We become attuned to these waves of energy like the waves in the ocean. We are opening up to the ten dimensions. As we move into peace, love, and harmony, we move out of hatred, greed, and control. But time takes time.

Although it feels as though hatred still has a stronghold on humanity, it is really just the last gasping breath of a dying false belief system. It is a culture that puts money before people. It is a culture that puts blame on others rather than taking responsibility for the actions, and consequences of self-serving greed.

The young ones will not live that way. They are making their voices heard right now saying, "No More!"

Every soul on the planet has the opportunity to see what really matters in one's life. This great awakening has increased the love energy in ways we could never have imagined.

There is something so dynamic that happens when one heart connects to another. That energy of love continues to thrive whether we meet again in moments or lifetimes.

Wow! That's stunning.

The elders and young ones who understand and encourage peace, love, and harmony are leading the charge into a new world. But change can only occur when we know what needs to be changed. Clearly, this is a time when people realize that words and actions have consequences. So, these must reflect gentleness and compassion to be seen and heard.

Decades from now, humanity will look back at this time and wonder how any of us could have lived in a world filled with so much vitriol and hatred. That's why it's a really good idea to stay healthy, and be here to share in the return to total love.

ABOUT ME

I write books! Novels, devotionals, kids' books, cookbooks, and screenplays. It's my passion. It's why I breathe. It's my service to humanity. I know the revealing power of words. Whether they are spoken or written, a single word can change the intended meaning.

My career path has included newspaper reporter, speech writer, author, screenwriter, and professor.

Words give us the power to speak the truth, and always, "less is more."

I believe a printed page is a picture. Words have a melody with texture and energy as well as meaning. As the words come together, it's like a concerto being played by an orchestra. The tone and cadence, the crescendos, the de-crescendos become part of the fabric of the story.

So, as you read these daily affirmations, I encourage you to listen with your spiritual ear. Pause and reflect. Feel them. Allow the words to speak to your heart.

May your days be filled with love and blessings beyond measure.

~ ND

ACKNOWLEDGEMENTS

A special thank you to Littel Industries for permission to use some of the wisdom of The Storyteller throughout this book.

5 August - David Viscott. Permission Requested.

11 August - Chinese Proverb. Public Domain.

12 August - Plato. Public Domain.

19 August - Lakota Prayer. Public Domain.

22 August - Mark Twain. Public Domain.

25 August - Pablo Picasso. Public Domain.

27 August - Nikola Tesla. Public Domain.

29 August - Sir Anthony Hopkins. Permission Requested.

11 September - Barack Obama. Public Domain.

14 September - Audrey Hepburn. Permission requested.

21 September - Solomon ben Judah, 11th Century Poet. Public Domain.

22 September - Charlie Mackesy, Permission requested.

5 October - Mahatma Gandhi. Public Domain.

8 October - Nikola Tesla. Public Domain.

17 October - Chuck Chamberlain. Public Domain.

22 October - Wallace Black Elk. Public Domain.

24 October - Storypeople. Used with permission.

4 November - President Joseph R. Biden, Jr. Public Domain.

10 November - Mark Twain. Public Domain.

21 November - Mark Twain. Public Domain.

15 December - Oscar Wilde. Public Domain.

23 December - St. Augustine. Public Domain.

30 December - Chief Seattle. Public Domain.

15 January - Sister Mary Ignatia. Public Domain.

19 January - Dolly Parton. Permission requested.

21 February - Charlie Mackesy. Permission requested.

29 February - Audrey Hepburn. Permission requested.

4 March - Storypeople. Used with permission.

4 April - Dr. Martin Luther King, Jr. Permission requested.

14 April - Audrey Hepburn. Permission requested.

22 April - Native American Proverb. Public Domain.

6 May - Richard Wagamese, Ontario, Canada. Permission Requested.

8 May - Mark Twain. Public Domain.

15 May - George Bernard Shaw. Public Domain.

17 May - Richard Wagamese, Ojibway, Canada. Permission Requested.

8 June - Aztec Indian Prayer. Public Domain.

13 June - Joy Harjo, Muscogee Nation. Permission Requested.

15 June - Anthony Brandt. Permission Requested.

20 June - Chief Joseph. Public Domain.

28 June - Mark Twain. Public Domain.

30 June - Kent Monkman, Canadian First Nation, Permission Requested.

1 July - President John Adams. Public Domain.

5 July - President Theodore Roosevelt. Public Domain.

6 July - Mark Twain. Public Domain.

8 July - Richard Wagamese, Ojibway, Canada. Permission Requested.

11 July - President Barack Obama. Public Domain.

14 July - President Dwight D. Eisenhower. Public Domain.

15 July - James Riddle Hoffa. Public Domain.

We have made every effort to contact the appropriate sources of these attributions. If we have overlooked giving proper credit to anyone, please accept our apology. Should any discrepancies be found, the publisher welcomes any written documentation supporting the correction for future publications.